1,401
Things That

P*SS
Me Off

1,401
Things That

P*SS
Me Off

I. M. Peeved

Developed by
The Philip Lief Group, Inc.

A Perigee Book

Perigee Books
are published by
The Putnam Publishing Group
200 Madison Avenue
New York, NY 10016

Library of Congress Cataloging-in-Publication Data

Peeved, I. M.
1,401 things that p*ss me off / by I. M. Peeved.
p.   cm.
ISBN 0-399-51670-0 (acid-free paper)
1. American wit and humor.   I. Title.   II. Title: 1,401
things that p*ss me off.   III Title: One thousand four
hundred and one things that p*ss me off.
PN6162.P356   1991   90-20326 CIP
818'.540208—dc20

Printed in the United States of America
9 10

This book is printed on acid-free paper.
∞

Introduction

The end is near. American culture has never faced a greater threat than it does right now. No, it's not toxic waste; it's not Richard Nixon's return; it's not even Jim and Tammy Faye Bakker. What heralds the onset of our nation's final days is the enormous success of that frighteningly cheerful and chillingly pathological list of things cute and nice that has seduced the American public. But happily, you are holding in your hand an antidote to all that wholesome sweetness.

1,401 THINGS THAT P*SS ME OFF comes to the rescue. A welcome relief from fuzzy kittens, rainbows, and all the other NICE things a certain best-selling book would like us to be happy about, this brilliantly nasty (if I do say so myself) compendium of life's everyday aggravations is designed to restore the country's mental health and revive good old-fashioned American cynicism.

So good-bye, raindrops on roses! *Auf Wiedersehen*, crisp apple strudel! I have Muzak on my mind. And waiting at home for a delivery.

And slow drivers in the fast lane. These chronic irritations—and some 1,398 more—are here for you to share and snarl over. I trust you will find some that have plagued you for years—and others you might never have come across till now. The perfect antidote to sappiness, 1,401 THINGS THAT P*SS ME OFF is one thing to be—at last—genuinely happy about.

—I. M. Peeved

slow drivers in the fast lane

cling wrap that refuses to cling

bad sex

public telephones that don't work

forgetting where you parked your
car

when your umbrella goes tulip in
the pouring rain

hearing the high school marching
band practice

people who *constantly* interrupt

when you buy a dozen eggs and
one is cracked

pits in the peach pie

when someone sits right next to
   you on an empty bus

not being able to lift the suitcase
   after you've packed it

losing on a game show

when the key breaks off while
   you're opening a can of sar-
   dines

when your socks fall down into
   your boots

locking the keys in the car

PBS fund-raising drives

when the bike chain falls off going
   uphill

Muzak

when the money machine eats your
   cash card

doctors who say, "this won't hurt a
 bit"

New Jersey's claim that it's the
 Garden State

recorded telephone solicitation

bank pens that don't work

wrong numbers at 3:00 A.M.

people who clip their nails in public places

rubberneckers

aerobics instructors who say, "you did very well . . . for a beginner"

when the sugar in the bowl hardens

having to refile your insurance forms because you left out your middle initial

waiting at home for a delivery

knowing your mate's asleep when
   you're still awake

anything polyester

when the shortest line at the checkout counter takes the lon-
   gest—and you're on it

when your alarm clock goes off and
   it's still dark outside

when the temperature won't adjust
   in the shower

toothpaste tubes squeezed from
the middle

squeaky doors when you're trying
to be quiet

zippers that get stuck

an out-of-order sign on the only
public bathroom around

trains on a holiday schedule when
you're not

small, thin books that cost $5.95

newsprint on your hands

hairdressers who do what they
   want, not what you want them
   to do

people who snap their gum

rental cars that break down

Millie, the White House Dog, being passed off as an author

when a section is missing from the
Sunday paper

cleaning the oven

white patent-leather shoes with
buckles

Brady Bunch reunions

running out of dental floss after
   you've eaten corn on the cob

when your parents forget your
   birthday

receiving a chain letter

when the flip-top breaks off your
   last beer

coffee from the bottom of the pot

oral surgery

sticking to plastic furniture in hot
weather

turkey roll

dropping your toothbrush in the
cat box

smiley faces

stepping in a slush puddle that
looks like solid ice

---

leaky paper coffee cups

trying to get from one airport ter-
   minal to another

when you can't find what you want
   in the refrigerator

five consecutive days of rain

waiting on a long line for a bad
   movie

buying a new electronic gadget that doesn't work

Olivia Newton-John

train conductors who announce, "there will be a slight delay"

state car inspections

greasy silverware in a restaurant

dentists with bad breath

when the dry cleaner charges by
the pleat

more books about "recovery"

dried-out meat loaf

Dan Quayle

when someone crackles a candy
wrapper behind you in a movie
theater

the end of daylight saving time

when your clothes wrinkle before
you get to work

getting hit by bird-do

sitting down on wet outdoor furniture

hangovers

an empty roll of toilet paper in the
   bathroom

when rabbits eat your garden

oil spills

dripping faucets

when it starts to rain five minutes
   after you arrive at the beach

people who jingle change in their
  pockets

when a sock gets lost in the wash

butter that's too hard to spread

stepping on chewing gum

finding the mug you bought on vacation has broken in your suitcase on the way home

bank pens on short chains

slow swimmers in the fast lane

taking your phrase book to a restaurant where nothing in the
book is on the menu

people who forget the punch line

lite potato chips

discovering the cheese you wanted for lunch is moldy

the feel of a motel carpet on bare feet

when the baseball game is rained out

knowing you're only going to get four hours of sleep

heavy briefcases

Yankee stubbornness

trying to clean a hollow-stemmed
    pilsner glass

getting the wrong directions

finishing all your snacks before the
    movie even starts

the D.A.R.

hat hair

deciding on new shoes

dentists who expect you to carry
    on a conversation with a
    mouthful of novocaine and
    cotton

when it's 95° outside but the water
    is freezing

discovering that your spouse sold
    your favorite hat for 12¢ at a
    yard sale

barstools with one short leg

February nights

getting three copies of the same
catalog in the mail

O'Hare airport in the winter

being at a boring party where
there's not enough to eat or
drink

a worm hole in your apple

crowded elevators

having a run of bad luck

when the refrigerator breaks down
in midsummer

when there's no cream for the coffee

when the gas station attendant
leaves your gas cap off

church bells ringing when you
have a hangover

Milford, Connecticut

the cost of Filofax date books

long winter weekends with nothing to do

trying to move a wheelbarrow
that's too full

when someone laughs at you

mowing the lawn when it feels like
you just did it

getting lost on winding roads

when the neighbor's dog barks
every time you pass by

losing your "things to do" list after
the first item is crossed off

trying to get your morning coffee
at a hotel

the small, sharp piece of lid that
the electric can opener missed

addresses that don't line up with
the window in the envelope

soggy cereal

getting a good idea and forgetting it before you write it down

when one card is missing from the deck

when the waiter mixes up the regular and decaffeinated coffees

when your favorite TV program is canceled because of a National Geographic special

finding that all the crackers are soggy

realizing you're out of shampoo
   after you step into the shower

pigeons mating

shrink wrap that's too tight to open

static electricity

when performers at live concerts
   lip-sync

seeing the TV you just bought ad-
   vertised for $100 less

when the thin red string you pull
    to open a Band-Aid breaks off

rubber boots that leak

nonfat ice cream

uninvited guests

people who don't "get" your jokes

putting on a cold, wet bathing suit

burning your fingers on a hot potato

cleaning up after a party

paper cuts

staples that break apart while you
are putting them in the stapler

when someone asks you for a
favor—and then nags you to
do it

when your favorite shoes get wet
and then shrink

knowing you have to go to the den-
tist

Vanna White, author

falling out of a hammock

going to bed when you know you
won't fall asleep

TV ads made to look like home
  videos

when the smoke from the grill
  blows in your face, no matter
  what side you stand on

creative visualization

low-fat cheese

losing your glasses

when the index gives you the
    wrong page number

detours

fruit that goes bad two days after
    you buy it

cat hairs in your coffee mug

when the wind picks up just after
    you finish raking the lawn

whistling teapots that don't whistle

when the dishwasher doesn't get the gunk out from between the fork tines

when the mail carrier delivers someone else's mail to your house

to*mah*to instead of tomato

when people say, "you cut your hair"

when raccoons get into the garbage

when it's 50° and cloudy in June

people who say, "smile, it can't be
    that bad"

busy signals

scraping your knuckle across the
    cheese grater

Milli Vanilli

bald babies who wear hair ribbons
   (around their whole head)

flat soda

sitting on gum

communal dressing rooms

trying to catch a taxi in the rain

a student loan going into its third
   decade

sour milk

rest room doors that don't lock

doing the bunny hop at weddings

liver spots

getting stuck with a damp towel
after a shower

poison oak

the "smile in the voice" of voice-
    over actors

surprise quizzes

forgetting to take your lens cap off

Spam

family-size Velveeta

people in a bank line who borrow
    your pen and forget to return
    it

Richard Simmons

Alf

forgetting your glasses when you
    go to a movie with subtitles

finance charges on credit card bills

wet wool

seat belts that tighten when you go
over each bump

waiters who keep asking if you are
done

lint balls

hollow chocolate bunnies

people who take a *really* long time
at the cash machine

mildew

getting a splinter

happy hours without hors
    d'oeuvres

know-it-alls

having to go through anything
    with a "fine-tooth comb"

changing the vacuum cleaner bag

ear wax

banging your shin on a metal bed
frame

scaffolding around landmarks

getting a bad fortune in a fortune
cookie

accidentally calling a fax number instead of a phone number

toilet paper stuck to the bottom of your shoe

forgetting to take your name tag off after a business convention

razor burn

getting soap in your eyes

fever blisters

"nonrefundable" deposits

not meeting the carry-on specifications at the airport

getting a tune stuck in your head for the whole day

losing money in a vending machine

dinner companions who can't
    make up their minds what to
    order

oat bran mania

"lemon fresh" anything

plastic coffee-cup tops you can't
    "notch"

no hot water

Shirley MacLaine

waiters who arrive with the entree
before you finish the appetizer

people who snack during phone
conversations

refolding road maps

people who continue to talk to you
while the water's running

getting into the car after it's been
sitting in the sun all day

when the tops of wooden matches
fly off like tiny comets

Sally Field

new acquaintances who automati-
cally shorten your name

book borrowers who don't return
the books

popcorn hulls stuck between your
teeth

people who say, "between you and
    I"

cleaning the stove

mosquitoes buzzing in the middle
    of the night

mosquitoes biting in the middle of
    the night

gunk on the windshield

hair brushes clogged up with hair

early morning construction outside your window

uneven table legs

sweater "pills"

dog owners who don't clean up
after their pets

advertising cards tucked under the
    windshield wiper

gum stuck under tables

flimsy paper napkins

aluminum foil against your fillings

strollers blocking the aisle

shoppers who bring twelve items to the "ten items or less" express line

rain right after you wash the car

when you only have last week's *TV Guide* on hand

cotton packed too tightly in aspirin bottles

forgetting to buy garbage bags—again

sticky movie-theater floors

flattened Junior Mints

dental floss that shreds when you
    use it

people who save every last piece of
    wrapping paper

elastic bands that break

greasy salt and pepper shakers

rosebuds that never open

junk mail made to look official

when the pay channel you DON'T
   subscribe to is showing the
   only watchable movie

programming the VCR

used Band-Aids in the sink

stupid outgoing phone messages

people smoking in the "no smoking" area

gritty spinach

warm beer

waiting for the delivery of take-out
food

men who don't aim

tasteless apples

dryers that eat socks and under-wear

getting sprayed by perfume demonstrators in department stores

holidays in the middle of the week

not having correct change for the bus

when your typewriter cartridge dies after the stores have closed

when there's no milk to have with the Oreos

putting something in a "safe place" and never finding it again

people who won't take a hint

having an itch where you can't scratch in public

leather furniture that makes embarrassing sounds

getting on a mailing list

friends who cancel at the last minute

people who just don't listen

having to resort to instruction
manuals

defrosting the refrigerator

being THE transfer student at a
  college reunion

congealed ketchup stuck in the
  neck of the bottle

a flat tire

sitting in the back row at a sub-
  titled movie

cities that roll up the sidewalks
  after 8:00 P.M.

finding a fingernail in your salad

little rat-like dogs

people who own little rat-like dogs

microwave cheese dip

spilling milk into the car's uphol-
    stery

cleaning the bug-zapper

allowing 4–6 weeks for delivery

when your hotel is packed with
   conventioneers

people who call it "the powder
   room"

guest towels

losing the hot water in the middle
   of a shower

needing more than two coats of
  paint

gritty hors d'oeuvre mussels

getting used to the ring of your
  alarm clock

cow tipping

finding a neatly folded, half-used
  sugar packet in a restaurant

the mechanical cheerfulness of
   ATMs

name dropping

squeaky shoes

when the coaster sticks to your
   glass

forgetting the punch line

rusty Brillo pads

when one piece is missing from a
jigsaw puzzle

muffins with scorched bottoms

people who refuse to learn your
schedule

cleaning the lint from the clothes
dryer

when somebody borrows one of
your Rolodex cards and
doesn't return it

Chinese restaurant music

shoe polish under your nails

clip-on bow ties

unreadable messages marked
"URGENT!"

people who refer to celebrities by
    their first names

chipping your favorite mug

waterbugs

getting the hiccups at the opera

a ten-teller bank with one teller on
    duty

four-dollar umbrellas

"adult" humor on greeting cards

when people set off Fourth of July
firecrackers from the first to
the tenth

when the tag of your teabag drops
into the hot water

the "clots" of old cream on the
surface of coffee

subscription cards that fall out of
magazines

new moms who drag their bawling
    infants to the movies

people who sing along with the
    tune

when you have to ask for water at
    a restaurant

painting window molding

getting caught in the middle of
    mutual friends' divorce

the obligatory "snarl-voice" of car ad spokesmen

the "stick 'em in anytime" style of late-night TV movie commercials

party guests who refuse to leave

typewriter keys that stick

hammering your thumb

the line to buy stamps at Christmas

finding your goldfish "belly-up"

being the only person out of costume at a Halloween party

folding fitted sheets

people who "burn rubber"

someone ahead of you in the cash-only line writing a check

when you lose five pounds and no-
body notices

having a nice bottle of wine but no
corkscrew

when the first crisis of the day oc-
curs before you're really awake

when that sweet old lady grabs
your cab

apartment hunting

neighbors who begin to party the moment you hit the sack

catching the bus—without exact change

relatives who ask, "so when are you getting married?"

one less payday in February

people who grab your "love handles"

kitty litter on your bathroom floor

hypersensitive smoke alarms

dealing with the soggy-food sludge
    left in the drain after washing
    the dishes

bus and train bathrooms

having to be a good sport

"return to sender—address un-
known"

closing the ring of a loose-leaf
binder on your finger

chatterbox hairdressers who need
both hands to express themselves

people who read aloud from the
newspaper

tuneless whistlers

running out of coffee filters

dirty city snow

dusting the knickknacks

people who borrow books, then
    return them with food
    smudges and folded corners

having a juicy sneeze without a tis-
    sue

discovering the hole in your pants
pocket at the END of the day

Ed McMahon's chuckle

dogs with bad breath

when your date falls asleep while
watching your favorite film

tube tops

charcoal briquettes that refuse to
    light

the dog's ear-piercing yelp after its
    paw has been stepped on

getting your stolen wallet back
    after you've canceled the
    credit cards

trimming your nose hair

rulers with ragged edges

being the last one chosen for a team

getting out the Christmas ornaments and finding your favorite one broken

waiting for the water to boil

losing the toggle-bolt inside the wall

sewing what you're mending to your pants leg

dry-swallowing pills

poking yourself in the eye with your eyeglasses

cleaning the hair from the shower drain

those rubbery blankets at motels

creamers with loose lids that dribble

watery shaving cream

drivers who don't use their direc-
tional signals

fuzzy V-neck sweaters (in fact, *any*
V-neck sweater)

people who snap their fingers for a
waiter's attention

cleaning the cheese grater

large golf umbrellas on a crowded
street

proselytizing

supermarket stickers on fruit

having to buy a CD player because
   records are obsolete

when the milk boils over the pan

charitable organizations that send
   solicitations every other week
   after you've contributed

when wealthy people complain
that they don't have enough

"gas" in church

when your mate breaks a promise

when people serve food and handle money at the same time

threading correction ribbon

strangers who don't say "thank you" after you've given them the time or held a door open for them

stores and boutiques that claim to have no rest rooms

cabbies who don't speak English

horseflies

doormen who don't open doors

waiters who tell you their names,
as if you care to have them join
you

boom boxes

people who take forever to get to
the point

voice-activated, computerized op-
erators

traffic jams

telemarketing sales reps

little dogs who wear hair ribbons

babies with nail polish and/or
    pierced ears

guilt

having to push a button to read
    your digital watch

John Denver

grown women who keep stuffed
   animals on their beds

"gourmet" cat food

getting lipstick on your shirt first
   thing in the morning

people who hand out flyers on the
   street

people who crowd through one
   door rather than go through
   the other available one

people who are perky in the morning

tie-dyed clothing

winter

cats that knock over the Christmas
tree

the new math

when your Rolodex cards get
    mixed up

a sudden storm when you're pic-
    nicking

getting only junk mail

the gap in the dressing room cur-
    tain that refuses to close

when the bag of M&Ms has mostly
    brown ones

feeling depressed

letting go of inhibitions and being
   told that you did so the next
   day

marine life that bites

when the public lavatory door
   hinge is broken

when the drive-in movie closes for
   the season

coffee stains on your teeth

dogs who smell your crotch

losing your umbrella

mothers who hit their kids for cry-
ing in public

when your favorite pajama pants
begin to fray

dripping wax

being all dressed up and having no
place to go

accidental meetings with people
you loathe

gnats

Tootsie Rolls stuck in your teeth

your mate's laundry hung on the
shower rod

people who are rich and taken care of

having to stretch to reach a parking lot ticket dispenser

when you can't figure out one word in the crossword puzzle

displayed collections in people's homes

the aroma of cinnamon rolls when you're on a diet

restaurants without liquor licenses

transit strikes

trying to get your landlord to paint
your apartment

spin-dry salad baskets that leave
the lettuce as wet as it was
when you put it in

driving against the arrow in a parking lot and confronting someone driving with the arrow

one-size-fits-all that doesn't fit you

rain during your vacation

deodorant that stains your clothes

lemons and limes with hardly any
juice

pencil lead on your fingers

trying to look up words you don't
   know how to spell

April Fools' Day jokes that really
   make a fool of you

sirens in the middle of the night

cleaning the gunk from ear plugs

the rat race

not being able to get to sleep on
   the train

the increasing price of postage
  stamps

scented cologne and perfume ads
  in magazines

losing your first love letter

the service charge on bounced
  checks

lumpy oatmeal

chores that you've got to do when you'd rather relax

taking a glass-bottomed boat ride and not seeing anything but seaweed

getting the giggles at a funeral

picking flowers, putting them between the pages of a big, heavy book to dry, and then forgetting them

losing your favorite recipe

the water that collects on the bottoms of mugs in the dish-
washer

flunking French for the fourth time

no-caffeine cola

when your pop-it beads pop all
over the floor

candy apples caught in your teeth

trying to make a purchase with foreign money

tangled phone cords

chewing gum in your hair

checkout clerks who don't know
what something is when you
buy it

a rainy evening alone

the aftertaste of a diet soft drink

dental floss trapped in your teeth

people who make you listen to an
   entire song before you get the
   beep on their message ma-
   chines

cabs that don't show up on time

dropping the andiron on your toe

scalding your tongue with the coffee

morning weather reports that turn
out wrong

losing five pounds one week and
gaining them back the next

dud fireworks

entrance fees

hamburgers served on pita bread

camphor-smelling sweaters

crumbs of toast left behind in the
butter

two-for-one sales where you can't
find anything you want

when your alarm clock doesn't
work

when your alarm clock does work

troublemakers

when your mother or father says,
    "no one else will ever love you
    the way I do"

having to button up button-fly
    jeans in a hurry

the 40-hour workweek

counting your blessings and finding none there

people who never postpone till to-
morrow what can be done
today

burning the marshmallows beyond
recognition

icicles that drop on your head

shorting out your at-home electric
buffet server

when you don't have the one spice
    you absolutely need

rug burns

when you get only bills in the mail

when adults say, "nighty-night"

waiting by candlelight for a special
    person who's an hour late

feeling compelled to go to a civic
    meeting

banks that don't open until 10:00
    A.M.

tulips blighted by a late spring
    frost

remembering when Hershey bars
    cost 10¢, hot dogs 50¢, and
    water was free

the common cold

having to invite over people you
    don't know or care about

discovering your hem has unrav-
    eled at work

salt rings on your shoes

a spot on your favorite tie

what humidity does to your hair

when your bra strap won't stay up

discovering that your vacation spot
    doesn't look at all the way it
    did in the brochure

rude swimmers in the lap lane

dust under your contact lenses

people who walk slowly three or
    four abreast along the sidewalk

smudges on your eyeglasses

soap scuzz in the bathtub

when food falls through the grill
   into the charcoal

breaking your favorite glass

rancid peanuts

corn silk left on corn on the cob

when the restaurant has no record
   of your reservation

being seated in the smoking section when you've requested
nonsmoking

gas station attendants who forget
about you

sitting next to someone with too
much perfume on

leaky pens

globs of ink from ball point pens

losing your car keys

when your companion wants to
talk about the movie before it's
over

raisin bran without enough raisins

when the soufflé falls

call waiting

misplacing the key to your diary

when the joke's on you

when the elastic gives out in your
  waistband

coming upon a new gourmet chocolate shop and not having a
  penny in your pocket

going to the health club only to be
  told the whirlpool is broken

getting an incomplete phone message

finding the safety-seal broken

remembering your diet after your
second bite of pie

running out of charcoal

trying on your summer clothes
after a long, lazy winter

forgetting everything you ever
    learned

trying to eat lunch on a park bench
    next to someone who is feed-
    ing the pigeons

losing your gloves

when your new flame exclaims,
    "wow, this is déjà vu" during a
    tender moment

being the only public school grad-
    uate at a party full of Ivy Lea-
    guers

ingrown hairs

soap too small to hold onto in the
    shower

those endless scar/operation/doc-
    tor conversations

people who always say, "so what's
    new?" or "what *else* is new?"

figuring out the restaurant bill at a
    table of seven people going
    Dutch

squeaky movie chairs

people who clap before the con-
cert is over

overhearing an uncomplimentary
remark about yourself

getting a flat tire on your way out
of town for vacation

low-fat pet food

being an adult and having a teen-
   age complexion

when people ask, "are you still
   with so-and-so?"—and you're
   not

losing a button

getting stuck at a railroad crossing
   when you're in a hurry

living west of your work

when the electricity goes out right after you've restocked the freezer

when the mustard packet spits its contents onto your shirt

spending all day fishing and not catching any fish

when people don't R.S.V.P.

not being able to get comfortable on the couch

when the coffee smells better than
it tastes

when more chocolate sprinkles
end up on your shirt than in
your mouth

when someone says you're not really looking your best

watered-down drinks

when the tall guy sits in front of
you at the movies

putting a shirt that's not colorfast
in with the white laundry

when people don't say, "excuse
me"

the fact that Rocky and Bullwinkle
are no longer on TV

driving to a party with a home-
made cake and losing the top
layer on the last curve

the shirt you stain every time you
wear it

biting your tongue

being more tired when you wake
   up than when you went to
   sleep

busses with worn "shocks"

politicians who say they won't raise
   taxes

when your mate doesn't shut the
   closet door

when your mate leaves the tooth-
    paste tube uncapped

when your mate forgets to turn the
    lights out

vitamins that stain your fingers

when there's nothing to eat for
    dessert

aromas stirring up memories
    you'd rather forget

losing a contact lens

arguing with your insurance company over a claim

getting lost on the back road you thought was a shortcut

people who make "I" the most frequent word in their conversations

breaking something a second time

yet-to-be-trained pets

when you insert a coin, but the
    parking meter doesn't register
    any time

not being able to find your way
    into your closet

dustballs

people who say you have to take
    the bad with the good

when you're counting on the car
lighter to work and it doesn't

hard-to-peel oranges

the sticky spots left on the wall
after you remove a picture

the misleading "light/dark" knob
on the toaster

people who hold open subway
doors

when someone tells you the whole
    plot before you finish the book

smudges on the windows after you
    clean them

when the car behind you honks to
    get you moving

clerks who don't know where
    something is in the store

ingrown toenails

when your knee goes out of joint

when someone uses the diminutive
form of your name that you
stopped using when you were
ten

the taste of glue on envelopes

scarring your new desk top

chairs that look great but are wildly
uncomfortable

hearing, "we're sorry, but your call
cannot go through as dialed"

when the dog climbs on the chair
it's not allowed on

taking out the garbage

restoking the wood-burning stove

sleep tapes that don't work

showing your embarrassment

cutting yourself with the bread
knife

not having enough cheese for your
taco

motel rooms that smell like bug
spray

when the doctor says the generic
brand won't do

blisters

the increasing price of Christmas
trees

when you're sitting by the edge of
the pool and someone splashes
you

diluted orange juice

when the root beer joints close up
for winter

burning when you only wanted a
little tan

that the E.R.A. didn't pass

static on the radio

losing everything you just did on
the computer

trying to clean the pan you forgot
and left in the oven overnight

bathing suits that ride up or slip off

condensation on the mirror in the
    morning

when the car battery goes dead in
    the parking lot

interjections

a blizzard in the spring

loudly ticking clocks

space heaters that worked last year
    but not this year

camping out without seeing a falling star

deadlines

squeaking clarinets

itching after playing outside in
winter

having to clean the toilet

"The Lord giveth; the Government taketh away"

flimsy paper plates

when your turn on line coincides
with a changing of the clerk

plastic knives

the parts of the windshield that the
wipers don't reach

the first bikini season following
   your pregnancy

truck headlights that illuminate
   your motel room at three in
   the morning

people who say, "a penny for your
   thoughts"

cavities

library fines

interrupted musings

not being able to get the bonfire
    going

required reading

when the soap dispenser in the
    dishwasher doesn't open

bad photos of yourself

losing your tickets to the sym-
phony

knowing you'll never have the figure you want

orange cats named Marmalade

slicing onions

bad vodka gimlets

waking up strangled by your paja-
mas

calorie charts placed at eye level
on the refrigerator

clams that won't open

having only your finger to stir the
coffee with

catcalls, hoots, and hollers

spot removers that don't work

having never yet cooked a steak to
    perfection

wrong numbers

carelessness

window shades that snap up in
    your face

planting seeds that don't come up

when the power goes out and you
    have to reset all the digital
    clocks in the house

unarguable fundamentals

when, in the middle of the night,
    the snow on the roof slides off
    with a thundering crash

the "upper crust"

not remembering whether or not
    you put sugar in your coffee

occupant mail

eager beavers

when the magazine instructions
leave out a step

getting in the wrong line at the
post office

being sadder but wiser

not being able to find things when
you need them

when the Cracker Jack box is missing the prize

car alarms

breaking the pencil point

dirty windows on the scenic train
   ride

compulsive crossword-puzzle
   doers

parting your hair crooked

Monday morning

burning the toast

picking the wrong lane in a traffic
   jam

realizing you forgot your towel
   when you get to the beach

slipping on ice

people who know exactly where
   they're going

waking up stiff

losing your place in the book

getting to the top of the World
   Trade Center and discovering
   it's too hazy to see anything

when what's in the box doesn't
   meet your expectations

having no place to wash your
   hands after eating cotton
   candy

people who talk too slowly

people who talk too fast

when the air-conditioning goes
   out at the health club

billboards along beautiful stretch-
es of highway

when the diskette has magically,
mysteriously, lost everything
overnight

overwatering the plants

when your nap is interrupted

bland chili peppers

when the window sticks shut

when you grease the window and
    then it won't stay open

mealy apples

dull knives

never having the time to read the
    books you want to read

getting fired

having to worry about salmonella in eggs

when a garage sale has nothing you want

that America has such a high illiteracy rate

when the airline loses your luggage

cutting your finger on the flip-top

scraping your knuckle along the
	cutting edge of the aluminum
	foil box

when the car air conditioner
	doesn't work

stepping on a slug with your bare
	feet

spilling your coffee all over your
	work

running out of ink mid-word

margarine in restaurants

pressing the wrong button on the
    computer and confronting a
    message you've never seen
    before and don't know how to
    decipher

feeling faint when the nurse draws
    even the tiniest bit of blood

scuffing your brand-new white ten-
    nis shoes

the piercing squeak your file
drawer makes every time you
open it

radios at the beach

that stale smell in your sink

when the toothpaste tube splits

when you can't get to the movie
before it leaves town

lawyers

when the sump pump breaks

when your knee-high's fall down

not getting a single valentine on
Valentine's Day

when someone forgets your name

trying to find your way around sta-
dium parking lots

being caught in a traffic jam when
you have to pee

the person who always has to have
the last word

corkboards that crumble

shoulds

trying to get the first drops of
ketchup onto your plate, not
the table

when your wishes don't come true

avocado seeds that don't sprout

Christmas commercialism

the stains on the coffee mug

all the talk about skin cancer ruin-
    ing the summer

not finding any books worth buying at a library sale

kinks in the garden hose

Japanese beetles

not being able to get the ball
   through the windmill in minia-
   ture golf

showers that are too hard

showers that are too soft

glove compartments that won't
stay shut

the demise of the ice cream truck

slopping soup on your shirt

when the repair people don't know
what they are talking about

not being able to thread the needle

losing half the contents when you
   open the bottle of champagne

when you pick up the phone and
   the caller hangs up

writer's block

when you always lose at cards

when you have to refill the mower
   with gas just a few feet short of
   the end of the lawn

mold in unexpected places

not having enough eggs for the recipe

when the microwave is on the fritz

not being able to find the toe clippers when you need them

the gray look of snow in the city an hour after it's fallen

being successfully conned

when your child reorganizes the
stacks of paper on your desk

when the cleaning person reorganizes your desk

billionaires

not having enough room on your
desk

unlisted phone numbers

washed-out bridges

when you know what you're
    breathing can't be good for
    you

breaking the antique glass inkwell

having to tear out the seam

being told you'd feel much better
     if only you stood up straighter

drafts

when the suitcase handle tears off

the zillions of Styrofoam wads that
     accompany mail-order items
     and end up all over the floor

painting the room and realizing
     it's absolutely the wrong color

committees of Congress

wrinkles in your suit pants

slow filling-station attendants

when you get to the store just as
they're closing the doors

Mensas

taking a lot of pictures and then finding there was no film in the camera

the ever-spiraling cost of pizza toppings

discovering that there is no real difference in the various cycles of your washing machine

people who say, "go for it"

not discovering you've mismatched your socks until you get to work

valentine candy hearts not tasting
   as good as they did in childhood

when the car rental office has
   never heard of you

knowing you'll never have the bi-
   ceps you want

not getting anything done

when the "spicy" chicken turns out
   to be bland

removing staples

botching a gourmet dinner

staticy airplane blankets

when you can't find a parking
  space

getting back to exercise

when you lose the muscle tone in
two weeks that took four
months to develop

when the down comforter loses its
fluff

when the coffee machine doesn't
work

when the ride turns out not to be
worth the trouble

Howard Johnson's coffee

smiling at people who never smile
back at you

waiting for the light to turn green
after noticing an empty parking spot across the intersection

when there are no pillows left on
the plane

when it's too cold on the plane

when it's too hot on the plane

ice-cream cones that leak

when your carry-on luggage
    doesn't fit in the carry-on
    space

conviviality when you're feeling
    blue

acquiescence when you're looking
    to fight

burning the bacon

the spots the sun screen misses

people who constantly click the
    clicker at the top of a ball-point
    pen

not being able to read the fine
    print

when the bartender forgets the
    maraschino cherry

questionable sheets in a motel

shin splints

peeling off a Band-Aid

cleaning the bird cage

stirring up the dust in your room

unreliable wristwatches

clock faces you can't read

people who jump to conclusions

highway patrols who hide at the
side of the road

stale dinner rolls

the cost of good red wine

losing your childhood snow shakers

trying to negotiate cobblestones
when you're wearing high
heels

when there's no room in the hammock for you

feeling cranky

carrying a rabbit's foot and still
having bad luck

losing your lens cap

when your good luck socks don't
work

having to say anything just to keep
a conversation going

pottery mugs that are cracked

not knowing the words to the
songs

leaves that drop before they turn

having to buy a gift for someone you don't like

pens that go through the wash

exam week

the smell of the city in the summer

not knowing who the Oscar win-
ners are

medical kits that have nothing use-
ful in them but Band-Aids

eight-lane freeways

electricians who overcharge

people who yell, "moo!" every
time they pass a cow

when one wheel on a shopping cart
   won't cooperate

soggy pretzels

raising corn that the woodchucks
   eat

self-threading needles that don't
   thread

filet mignon, overcooked

secondhand stores that charge more for the clothes than when they were new

getting halfway across the sand and realizing it's too hot for bare feet

wrinkles around your eyes

women who dress for aerobics class in dangling earrings, coordinated outfits, and full makeup

hamburgers with mustard, lettuce, tomato, pickle, onion, and cheese at 10:30 A.M.

two-pound tubs of margarine

overpriced condominiums

Continental breakfasts with only
one roll

child geniuses

handicraft centers in New England
that overcharge

food you forgot you had in the
   root cellar until you could
   smell it

politicians

a moth hole in your favorite
   sweater

being called for jury duty

working for a stickler for details

not having enough cash on hand

oil lamps with short wicks

rain slickers that leak

squeaky cars

cutting the cloth when cutting tags
   off new clothes

hay fever

using a thimble and still pricking
    yourself

snow when you're already late

seven-and-seven drinks

having a heart-to-heart with Dad

reading a bad book

getting home and finding the eggs
    you just bought are outdated

getting home and finding the milk
    you just bought is outdated

getting home and finding the meat
    you just bought is outdated

your favorite records scratched

sprained ankles

trees blowing over in a storm

mushrooms at $15.95 an ounce

"soda parlors" that charge for
water

cotton clothes that shrink in the
wash

people who hold the elevator
   doors

tablecloths that don't fit the table

stained pillowcases

allergies

chipping your bone china

not being able to avoid people who
    make you feel guilty

getting a hangover from two
    glasses of wine

people who can't make up their
    minds

stupid questions

being shortchanged

dry toast

Western Civ. classes

tracking mud through the house

cold hands

not being able to find a briefcase
that doesn't look like everybody else's

shaving wounds

when the salt shaker cap comes off

getting the sugar/cream level of
    your coffee just right only to
    have a waiter come along and
    ruin it

hypochondriacs

when the car heater doesn't work

the one leaf that remains caught in
    the rake

cold feet

mirrors that distort you

finding out that you need glasses

getting locked in a bathroom

hospital gowns

the meaning of existence

losing a race

when you haven't got a Kleenex in
   the car

the seven virtues: charity, faith,
   fortitude, hope, justice, pru-
   dence, temperance

eyes without hooks

bakery boxes so tightly tied with string that you can't sneak in for a fingerful of frosting

always being the one to get up first and make coffee

answering the phone just as the machine picks up

the kid who got the Rhodes scholarship

the fence blocking the view of the garden

when the bubble gum pops in your face

duck motifs

when the fuzz on tennis balls wears off

people who say they never watch television

when you're dying for a cup of coffee and the waiter says, "it'll be just a minute; a new pot has to brew"

people who think they sing as well
  as Aretha Franklin

not being able to fix your toaster

when your sneakers are still wet
  after running them through
  the dryer

when your mate takes forever to
  dress

being too pale to go out in the sun

ennui

being stranded in an airport

not being able to throw a football
through a tire

slush

a penny blocking a 5¢ gumball slot

chronically underrating your own
abilities

pouring milk into a cereal bowl
and having the cereal spill over
the edge

the way condos have blighted the
landscape

leaving spaces in your day to do
something spontaneous and
then finding nothing to do

opening an aerogram

people who snap you with rubber-
  bands

stiff sheets and pillowcases

climbing to a lookout point and
  finding the view obstructed

flip-down airplane trays that have
  leftover food on them

armless chairs

people who act like experts on a
    topic after having read only
    one article in the newspaper

when the tennis court lights go out

boring letters

being caught when you're trying to
    get away with something

when the elevator lurches

people who say, "where there's a
will, there's a way"

when the muffin sticks to the paper
holder

sneers

a case of the sniffles

straight-backed chairs

snobs

snooty people

when your mate snores

not having the correct postage

noisy, souped-up cars

when the dog chews the phone
cord in half

floating downriver in a leaky inner-
tube

peeling a hard-boiled egg and losing half of the white part

decaf espresso

breaking ice cubes out of the tray and finding they're not quite frozen

tasteless tomatoes

missing the basket at an exact-change toll booth

burnt toast

fish bones in your soup

being an understudy

another project left uncompleted

grabbing at straws

expecting the worst and getting it

spraying your hair with deodorant

lost causes

wild goose chases

more numbers added to zip codes

the sound of cats eating

the three-second delay in an over-
    seas phone conversation

the fine layer of grease and dust
behind the stove

pulling the cord completely out of
drawstring pants

walking into unseen spider webs
across the sidewalk

undercooked rice

oozing, overstuffed egg-salad sand-
wiches spilling on your pants

wearing the eraser down before
   the pencil is used up

waxy European toilet paper

being tickled by someone you hate

torn currency

lambies and bunnies in the
   butcher's window

no counter space in the kitchen

runny stenciling

bare feet on hot asphalt

cabinets that have become bug
    cemeteries

being referred to as "Hey, you!"

no chimney for Santa Claus

cheap Lucite furniture

worrying about loose dentures

skating on thin ice

nothing but novelty gifts for your
    birthday

the effects of acid rain

invisible stains that show up after
  dry cleaning

hangnails

detention hall

ducking and still hitting your head

what the tide did to your sand cas-
  tle

unreadable messages on valentine
    candy

carrying a torch

greasy oven mitts

impacted wisdom teeth

soggy playing cards

discovering miles of toilet paper in
the trees in your front yard

self-service-only gas stations

a romantic holiday all by yourself

the color of overmixed, overused
modeling clay

sleepyseeds in your eyes

the people who hang around railroad stations

untangling chicken wire

Bob without Ray

reaching out to unreceptive people

pet puke

waiting for Mr./Ms. Right

getting your car towed

no cherries in the fruit cocktail

drinking from a finger bowl by
mistake

blunt toenail clippers

strong waves and a loose bathing
suit

pool chlorine up your nose

spaghetti again

cracks in the ceiling widening

plastic "wicker" furniture

a tiny, almost undiscoverable hole
    in the air raft you've been
    blowing up

kissy-noise phone static

starting a highly recommended
    book for the fourth time and
    still not being able to finish it

unnatural potpourri scent and
    color

dropping a favorite magazine in
    the toilet

no Tootsie Roll center in the Toot-
    sie Roll Pop

playing badminton on a windy day

that one overlooked stay-pin in a
    new shirt

having to wait for an answer

having to moonlight

wet, clammy porch swings

being the black sheep at a family
gathering

swollen ankles

undercooked chicken

shaking a bottle of salad dressing
with a loose cap

stepping in dog-do

wobbly restaurant tables

pouring spoiled milk on your cereal

obligatory family visits

shoveling wet snow

the sound of a mosquito right by your ear

bus exhaust

getting cut off by an answering machine

customer service personnel who act like they're doing you a favor

celebrities you never heard of

pre-ripped jeans for $80 a pair

William F. Buckley

dealing with the grease after you
   fry bacon

drivers who sneak up the lane
   that's blocked and then expect
   you to let them into the open
   lane

taking the time to pack a lunch and
   then forgetting it at home

pouring a cup of coffee and not
   having time to drink it until it's
   cold

penny loafers with foreign coins in them from the country the wearer last visited

buying a bag of pistachios and finding most of the shells impossible to open

people who argue over whether Rhett and Scarlet ever got back together

buying tickets way in advance and then finding out the day before the event that you can't go

people who read over your shoulder

pot-luck dinners where everyone
brings a macaroni salad

shower massages that don't work
anymore

hitting your funnybone

having to "go Greyhound"

scooter drivers who don't obey
traffic laws

when your desk gets moved next to the copier machine

feeling too tired after work to do what you had been looking forward to all day

having to do something "for your own good"

when you turn on the TV to watch a show you've only seen once before and it's the same episode

Miss Manners

being quoted incorrectly

feeling manipulated

needing a tow truck to pull your
     four-wheel drive out of a snow-
     bank

people who frequently toss foreign
     phrases into their conversation

surcharges

getting your pants leg stuck in the
    bike chain

seeing someone you wanted to im-
    press on the street when you
    look your worst

finding exactly what you wanted
    and then being told the store is
    out of your size

when the board of health closes
    down your favorite diner

getting overcharged for something
    that's already expensive

being eliminated in the first round

forgetting your sweater on a cool
night

jumping over a puddle and missing

slowly dying houseplants

low water pressure

people who spit on the sidewalk

biting into unpopped popcorn

trying to use a shoe to hammer a
nail into the wall

finding a new resort hotel on your
favorite isolated beach

the third opinion that thoroughly
confuses you

suntan oil on your bathing suit

forgetting to turn the oven on

forgetting to turn the oven off

when both sides of the reversible
    place mat are stained

glasses that pinch your nose

sale racks with nothing on them
that you'd want to buy

when you walk the dog and it won't
do anything

unproductive periods

when the vacuum won't pick up the
dirt

intolerably hot days

intolerably cold days

not remembering the last time you
   had the chance to sleep in

when your old calfskin wallet fi-
   nally wears out

the button at intersections marked
   "push to cross"

opening the wrong side of the milk
   carton

making a mistake when trimming
your own hair

skating parties when you don't
skate

discovering how far back you are
on the take-a-number line

people who say, "hunky-dory"

half-baked people

leaving your umbrella on the train

people who are up and outdoors
    while the day is still young and
    damp with dew

working too hard and not getting
    paid for it

trying to pick the corn silk off the
    floor after husking the corn

when you haven't received a letter
    from your old college room-
    mate in years

lumpy mattresses

Astroturf

rancid buttercream frosting

people who talk baby talk to babies

people who say, "nice doggie"

bad enchiladas

midnight phone calls

melting snow that makes impass-
    able streams

falling asleep on the lawn and wak-
    ing up with an allergy head-
    ache

bad popcorn

being a night person and living
with a morning person

the way the car windows intensify
the heat of the sun

people who chew ice

not being able to read your own
handwriting

waistbands that carve rims into
your stomach

questionable restaurant food

pancakes with the batter still un-
cooked on the inside

time cards

being at a loss for what to do on
the weekend

when people use your floor for an
ashtray

losing half your food in your lap

borrowing more books from the library than your book bag will hold, then trying to negotiate your way home

when someone encroaches on your sense of space

when your date makes you sit through the credits

staying home on New Year's Eve

going out on New Year's Eve

New Year's Eve

discovering that your ex-spouse
has remarried

getting crayon on your hands,
shirt, shorts

when the phone goes dead

children's clothes with buttons instead of Velcro

PTA meetings

when the chiropractor goes on vacation

losing one earring

losing one cuff link

high boots on unexpectedly hot
    days

male chauvinist pigs

telephoning from overseas

bulldozers going outside your win-
    dow all day

sending a fan letter and getting no
    response

when the squirrels get in the bird feeder

show-offs

when the toaster breaks a day after the warranty period is over

when your jeans shrink more than you expected them to

when the couple you're dining with plays kissy-face all evening a leak in the water bed

dirty city parks

New York taxi drivers

unpadded bicycle seats

oven mitts that don't work

nonadjustable hairbands

being scolded for laughing

the bottom of the sundae glass that
    you can't reach with your
    spoon

discovering that your mittens
    haven't yet dried from the last
    snowball fight

the people who talk to characters
    in movies

when you can see how the magic
   trick was done

going someplace you've never
   been and discovering it was
   better left unseen

sinking your teeth into a fresh
   peach and discovering it's sour

wishing for a new car and knowing
   you can't afford it

discovering only twin beds in the
   motel room

eating only one slice of pizza and the next day discovering that you're a whole pound heavier

not living near public transportation

preventive medicine that fails

dining hall meals

when the store you like the best goes out of business

emptying the bug corpses from
light fixtures

when your nail polish chips

socks that are too short

recorded holiday music blared
across the streets of small
towns

rear-window defoggers that don't
work

people who speak loudly to for-
eigners as if to make themselves   more   readily
understood

when the day slips away

not being able to do a cartwheel

when something is too heavy to
carry

being the last one asked to dance
at a party

when the mail carrier steps on the
    first crocus

chatty people when you'd rather
    sulk

wicked jacks players

clouds on the night of the full
    moon

cabin fever

the questionable dark ring around
the bottom of soda-pop bottles

jammed View-Masters

the fact that the Christmas season
now starts the day after Halloween

hospital food

pinching your finger in the folding
chair

being put on hold for twenty minutes

being photographed when you
   don't want to

when the cat knocks over the
   flowerpot

when a dog brushes against your
   clean suit pants

when the rubber door sweeps
   leave permanent marks on the
   floor

being too nervous to ask for an autograph and regretting it later

trying out for a game show and not making it

packets of free coupons offering discounts on nothing you need

not being able to find a comfortable position in bed

when there's not enough banana for the cereal

when the teeniest, tiniest sliver of
    wood is stuck beneath your
    nail

when the match won't light

people who talk through the movie

when the lamp you bought is deliv-
    ered broken

when there are no big waves

chemical-tasting water

losing one flip-flop

when you go back to look at your
old report cards and discover
your parents have thrown
them out

when the bath water is too hot

when the bath water is too cold

not being able to suck your stomach in far enough to fasten
your pants

when your glasses fog over

Imelda Marcos

not having a saucepan big enough
for the soup

throwing caution to the wind and
regretting it

insomnia

hard scrambled eggs when you
   asked for soft scrambled

when everybody else on the road
   can't drive

the strapless bra that won't stay up

when the rent-a-wreck you rent is
   really a wreck

belts that pinch your waist

shoes that pinch your toes

feeling like you don't deserve it

when your cold is so bad you can't
   taste anything

when you order something from a
   catalog and it doesn't look at
   all like it did in the photo

that one fly that won't desist

going out to buy yourself a treat
    and not being able to find any-
    thing you want

the fact that hitchhiking is too dan-
    gerous to do anymore

stale-tasting ice cubes

when your mate commandeers the
    Sunday paper to the bathroom

causing an avalanche of snow
 when you open the door

lint on Velcro

when there's no one to meet you at
 the airport

when the grocery bag breaks five
 blocks from home

people who look good in anything

when people insist on singing the
    second and third verses of
    "Happy Birthday"

unattended airport information
    booths

dogs that don't fetch

when the meter reader comes
    around at eight o'clock Satur-
    day morning

doctors

a bee in the car on the highway

being compared to someone you
really don't like

incomprehensible song lyrics

getting motion sickness

traveling with someone who gets
motion sickness

when the waiter asks how you want
      your burger cooked and then it
      isn't cooked that way

sitting in one airplane watching
      your luggage get loaded onto
      another

pep talks

living next to a would-be rock
      band

getting the flu on your vacation

people who refer to themselves in
the third person

the smell of cafeteria food in the
morning

departure taxes

screen doors that bang

Saddam Hussein

burning your hand on a handle
you didn't think was hot

losing the garage door opener

fruit flies

people who cheat at cards

buying unfinished furniture and
never getting around to painting it

having to compromise

thinking there's a second layer of
    chocolates underneath the first
    and being wrong

running out of brake fluid

headaches

flashlights with weak batteries

when you're outnumbered in the vote over the pizza toppings

dried-up saddle soap

forgetting to set the timer on the automatic electric coffee-starter

being constipated

when the dog eats all the cat food

introductory offers that cost more than the regular price

never having caught a baseball hit into the stands

when your sibling borrows your clothes—and looks better in them than you do

being put in a headlock

piano recitals

someone else's hairs on your soap

dried toothpaste on the sink

two pounds of packaging for one ounce of product

when none of the many pens in the drawer work

people who chew popcorn loudly during the movie

when you can't remember the last
time you looked terrific

when someone else points out that
you're getting wrinkles

stubbing your toe on the cracks in
the sidewalk

overpriced movie snacks

the day after a binge day

when none of the hiccup remedies
   work

moldy shower benches

when the sky is clear and clean,
   and the air is full of soot

disappointing croissants

when you don't get your change
   owed from a vending machine

public toilets that haven't been
   flushed

windshield wipers that smear

a clogged ketchup bottle that un-
   clogs suddenly on your food

plants that drip when you water
   them

lite beer

obnoxious morons who make
more money than you do

talk show hosts who talk more than
their guests

cat hair on your black suit

when the dishwasher leaves crud
on the dishes

a fly in the salad

realizing that you really need something you threw out last week

speed bumps

when you miss your exit and can't turn around for twenty miles

delayed green lights

when you open a soda bottle and it sprays all over

14,000 things to be happy about

losing your soap in the tub

people who wear mirrored shades

"baby on board" signs

when someone driving toward you
leaves their high beams on

Nixon's comebacks

people who don't give you a chance to get a word in edgewise

breaking a dish after you wash it

when you can't find what smells in the refrigerator

when the stairs squeak and it wakes up the baby

when your answering machine cuts off the end of a message

Are You Pissed?

Ever wish you could tell the whole world just how mad your boss makes you? Got a gripe about sentimental laxative commercials? Well, here's your chance to give a piece of your mind to everyone who bugs you. On the form below, tell us what really gets your goat. Or send us a whole list of annoyances that set you seething. Whether you fume about taxes or can't stand wire coat hangers, let us know. We might print your complaint in the next edition of this book, but then again, we might not. Either way, you won't get paid for it—but that just gives you one more thing to be pissed about. So get out your pencil and start kvetching. There's never been a better way to blow off steam.

Mail your list to: I. M. Peeved
c/o The Philip Lief Group, Inc.
6 West 20th Street
New York, NY 10011

_____

_____

_____

_____

_____

_____

If you enjoyed *1,401 Things That P*ss Me Off,* don't miss out on another hilarious book—*Bob Saget's Tales from the Crib* with Tony Hendra—coming soon from Perigee.